How to
Repair & Restore Dolls

How to
Repair & Restore Dolls

Barbara Koval

ROBERT HALE • LONDON

Dedicated to my family and friends who said 'Do it', and to my girls who have shown a gentle appreciation for all dolls—my daughter Sheri, my granddaughters Melinda, Allissa and Lara, my chosen granddaughter Gabby. If not for children like them there would not be the heritage of beautiful dolls we have today.

Acknowledgments

Special thanks to Perry Cooper for his great graphics, to Sheri Koval for all the printouts and preparation, and for photography to Sheree Kalousek.

ISBN-0-7090-4875-0

Robert Hale Limited
Clerkenwell House
Clerkenwell Green
London EC1R OHT

Printed in Hong Kong by Colorcraft Ltd

Contents

Introduction   6

1   You can do it   7
2   Cleaning and rejuvenating plastic and vinyl
      dolls   9
3   Replacing cloth bodies on modern plastic
      dolls   11
4   Restoring dolls' hair and removing and fitting
      wigs   19
5   Restringing composition dolls   24
6   Repairing and building up composition   29
7   Repairing plaster and papier-mâché   32
8   Bisque repairs   34
9   Pedigree and Cherub repairs   42
10   Repairing celluloid dolls   44
11   Restringing celluloid dolls   49
12   Painting   54
13   Resetting sleeping eyes   57
14   Endnotes   60
Where to find things   63
Index   64

Introduction

Looking back over the years it seems that dolls have always held a fascination for me. I made my first doll when I was eight years old, from an old handkerchief filled with straw, the first and only doll I was to own until the war ended in 1945.

My innate love of dolls has grown over the years, as has my collection of old dolls, broken, sorry, sad looking dolls. I have found them all irresistible. In the end it became necessary for me to learn (mainly by experimentation) how to restore my treasures.

Thousands of people all over the world love and collect dolls—maybe some of them, like me, will derive great pleasure from transforming a once broken and battered little doll to its original beauty. This book is written with these people in mind.

The doll I am holding brought so much joy to her owner after it had been restored. I dressed it exactly as she told me it had been when given to her when a child. These are the moments that make the task of doll repairing so rewarding (courtesy *Newcastle Herald*)

1 You can do it

So you have rescued or been given an unhappy looking plastic doll...you can see beauty under all that neglected but sometimes loving grime (as only a true doll-lover can). Where do you start? Come with me, we will make that doll live again.

We will advance to repairing all sorts of dolls, from plastic to bisque. If you are dedicated (and you must be to read this far), and you're adventurous, then in no time at all you will be repairing not only your own dolls but other peoples' as well.

I love old dolls, not for their perfection or for the amount of money they may bring, but for the grace of a bygone era, for their lifelike charm, and for the love that was once given to them. Some folk crave only perfection in a doll, perhaps seeing it as an investment which must be in mint condition. To me, mint condition means nothing — the enjoyment of seeing and touching a well loved doll is what collecting is all about in my eyes. Who cares if under ultra-violet radiation a repair can be detected? I look at dolls with a loving eye; if I can rescue that gem for posterity, flawless or not, I will. How can we allow such treasures to disappear?

I no longer collect dolls, having long since run out of room — not being able to display them for others to enjoy seems such a sin. I shudder over those zealous individuals who collect hundreds of dolls only to hoard

Twenty-five years after she first delighted my daughter at Christmas, the walking doll Pollyanna is still treasured, even though missing one leg

Three Australian dolls in near original condition

them away; some dolls in such collections never see the light of day. Such people amaze and sadden me. Thank goodness they are in the minority — most doll collectors love and appreciate their role as collectors; they are helpful and very considerate people. I hope you never become a doll tyrant.

Do you enjoy working with your hands? If the answer is yes, you are going to love my methods, as the only tool you will be using most of the time will be your hands. You need outlay very little money for tools as most will be found in and around your home. We are going to save money and have lots of fun along the way. You will learn not just one or two of my secrets, but all of them.

The most important thing is to read through the complete book carefully before attempting any repair, then study the chapter relating to the repair you wish to undertake. Make sure you thoroughly understand the correct use of materials and the method before proceeding — that way you will have only success, whether you are just cleaning your doll, removing biro from a much loved plastic or vinyl doll or restoring a precious antique. Together we will add another dimension to your doll collecting or lead you to a whole new career in doll repairing.

This toddler was missing her right leg

2 Cleaning and rejuvenating plastic and vinyl dolls

You will need: Nifty cleanser, baby oil, Oxy-10, toothbrush, cotton buds, plastic hair brush, clean rags

Cleaning should always be carried out without submerging the doll in water or any other liquid.

Nifty is a good all-round cleaner for this kind of work — it is not harsh, the results are very good, it is available from most supermarkets, and it gives excellent results on plastic or vinyl dolls. Arm yourself with a good supply of old soft clean cloths, old towels and old flannelette for polishing up.

To begin, soak a piece of towel well with Nifty. Working from top to bottom of doll, rub the Nifty into the surface, working on one part at a time. As soon as you have cleaned each part wipe it over with a clean damp rag, then quickly dry off with a larger piece of towel.

Make sure that you clean into the tiny crevices around the nose, mouth, ears and fingers — a soft toothbrush is ideal for this part of the job.

For cleaning the eyes use a cotton bud soaked with Nifty. Work very gently when attending to the doll's eyes, as some eyes balance on a very fine piece of plastic which can quite easily be broken.

By now the doll should be looking sparkling clean, just requiring that little something extra to bring her back to almost her original glory. For this part of the treatment I use baby oil — it's my magic oil. Having tested every known wax and polish over the years, baby oil has given 100% proven results.

Throughout this book almost all finishing is done using baby oil. I use it on plastic, vinyl, composition, celluloid and bisque. (Although I do not touch on wax restoration in this book I have had the same success there with baby oil, using it in a slightly different way.)

Going back to the cleaning process, pour 2–3 ml (about half a teaspoon) of oil onto a wad of soft cloth. Working quickly, rub into all parts of the doll, using a cotton bud for the eye area. Polish away any excess with a flannelette rag. You will be amazed at the difference. Is that really the same doll?

Baby oil not only imparts a natural sheen, it also helps to preserve dolls made from the old materials, appearing to control splitting and crazing. So often you will find the simple method produces the most rewarding results. The lustre you obtain with baby oil, especially on celluloid or Pedigree dolls, will delight you.

How many dolls have you seen discarded because of

unsightly biro marks covering their faces or bodies? Like me, no doubt, you have tried hairspray, peroxide, Brasso, bleach, spirits — the list goes on. I remove biro with the most unlikely product — Oxy-10 (available from your local chemist). Yes, it is a treatment for teenage skin complaints, but I use it for a skin treatment of a different kind!

For the best results remove biro marks before starting the general cleaning process. Apply a heavy coat of Oxy-10 directly onto each biro mark and put the doll aside for a week. At the end of this time just wipe off the Oxy-10 with a damp cloth. If any stain still remains repeat the application and leave for a second week. A second treatment is more often needed on modern plastics; for some reason the Oxy-10 works faster on older materials. Plates 2 and 3 on page 17 demonstrate the success of this method.

Warning: If you are using Oxy-10 to remove marks on the cheek area, use it sparingly as too heavy an application may remove some of the blush. When you are starting out on your very first repair it is only natural you will be apprehensive, so first try it out on a truly wrecked doll's head. This way you will find just how much you need to apply to blush areas.

3 Replacing cloth bodies on modern plastic dolls

You will need: calico, strong soft string, UHU glue, darning needle, surgical scissors (see page 13)

Doll repair, like any other craft, is basic common sense. In jobs such as replacing limbs you are going to have to use this common sense to make sure, for example, that all replacement limbs are going to point in the correct direction, that there are no left legs or arms where right ones should be. Go carefully and watch what you are doing each step of the way. It's maddening when a doll has been put back together and you heave a sigh of relief at a job well done to find that you have put a leg on backwards or worse. Carry out little checks throughout to make sure you are on the right track.

To make a new cloth body, first open up the back middle section of the old body for 13–15 cm (5–6 inches), as shown in Figure 3.1. Remove the filling and put it aside, discarding it only if the filling is soiled or you detect an unpleasant odour. Carefully cut off the fabric around the limbs and the head (Figure 3.2). Open up the seams of the old body (Figure 3.3) and press it flat to serve as a pattern for the new body, which you may replace with any material you choose. I prefer calico — it's durable, easy to sew and cheap.

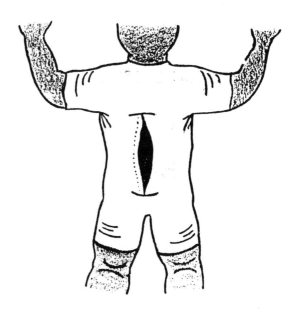

Fig. 3.1 Opening up the back of the cloth body

To cut out the new body simply follow the outline of the original body, remembering to add extra for the bits left behind when removing the head and limbs

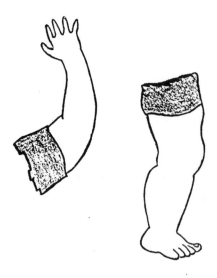

Fig. 3.2 Cut the fabric attached to the limbs (and head) as close to the joins as possible

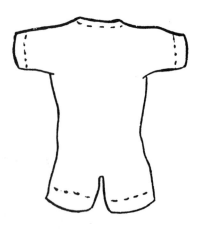

Fig. 3.4 The dotted lines indicate where extra fabric should be allowed when cutting the new body

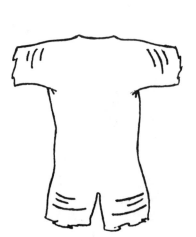

Fig. 3.3 Use the old body opened out for a pattern

(Figure 3.4). This part is very straightforward and should present no problems.

Sew around the fabric, leaving openings for arms, legs and head (Figure 3.5).

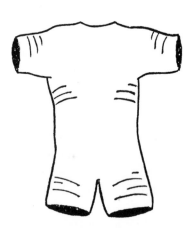

Fig. 3.5 The new body sewn up

Modern plastic dolls differ in the way the limbs are manufactured. Some dolls, such as Prince William, have no groove at the top of the limb (Figure 3.6). Dolls such as Vogue which do have the groove (Figure 3.7) are much simpler to work with.

In the case of the Prince William doll and others without the groove I have overcome the problem by making 8 to 12 holes around the top of the limb,

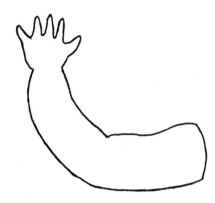

Fig. 3.6 Prince William-type arm—no groove

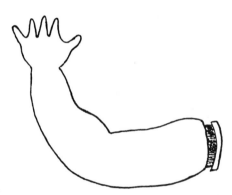

Fig. 3.7 Vogue-type arm is grooved

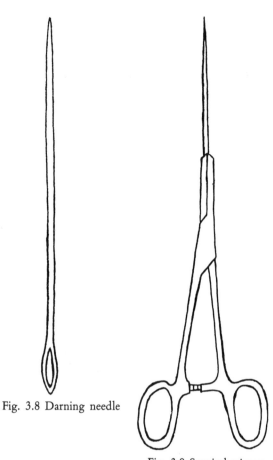

Fig. 3.8 Darning needle

Fig. 3.9 Surgical scissors

working about 1 cm (¼ inch) from the top. The holes are easily made using a hot needle. Make the holes just big enough for the needle you are using to pass through easily. A large darning needle (Figure 3.8) is ideal; heat the needle over a flame. Holding it with surgical scissors locked into clamp position (Figure 3.9), make holes as quickly as possible. Reheat the needle as necessary. Usually the head on this kind of doll is grooved (Figure 3.10), but if it has no grooves (Figure 3.11) use the same method as for arms and legs. A greater number of holes will be needed.

The next step is a thorough cleaning and oil treatment for the head and limbs (refer to Chapter 2). If the doll's

Fig. 3.10 Grooved head

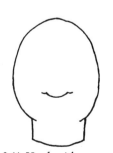

Fig. 3.11 Head with no grooves

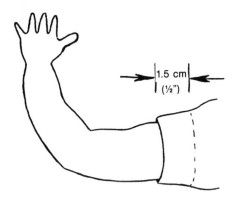

Fig. 3.12 Inserting right arm into armhole

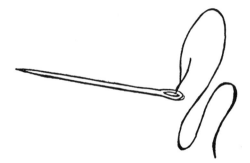

Fig. 3.13 Needle threaded with strong string

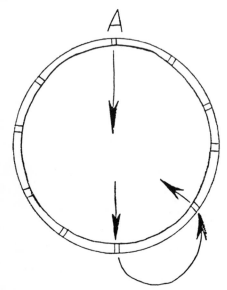

Fig. 3.14 Working the string through the holes in the arms, legs or head to attach the fabric

Fig. 3.15 The criss-cross pattern of working

Fig. 3.16 Finishing with a strong knot, leaving about 2.5 cm (1'') of string

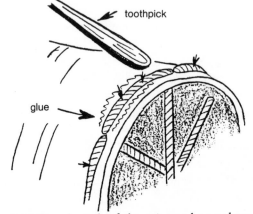

Fig. 3.17 Glue the ends of the string and press down with a toothpick

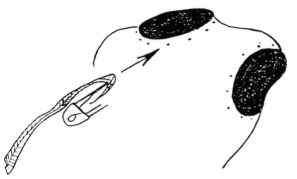

Fig. 3.18 Use a small safety pin to thread the string through the neck seam

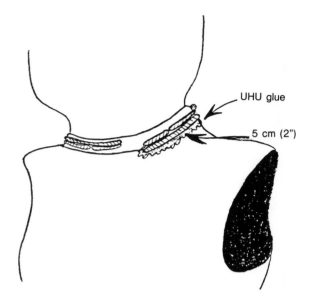

Fig. 3.20 Glueing down the ends of the string

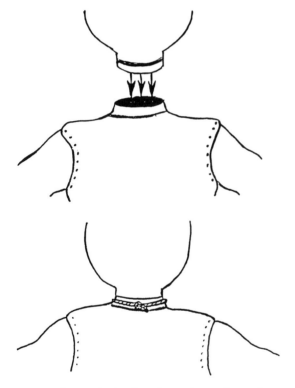

Fig. 3.19 Placing the head in the neck opening and tightening the string

hair also needs to be restored, do that next, referring to Chapter 4.

Now armed with the new body turned right side out we are ready to assemble the limbs. Working from the right side, insert right arm into armhole, turning back 1.5 cm (½ inch) of arm fabric (Figure 3.12). You now begin to work within the body section of the doll. Using the strong string (Figure 3.13), and starting at point A (Figure 3.14), attach the fabric to the head/arm/leg, working in and out in a criss-cross manner until all holes have been used (Figure 3.15). Tie a secure knot leaving about 2.5 cm (1 inch) of string remaining (Figure 3.16). Apply a generous quantity of UHU glue along the ends of the string, and press them down with a toothpick (Figure 3.17). UHU is a great adhesive for this type of work, being quick drying and having good holding qualities. UHU can be found at art shops and some newsagents. Working in the same manner, attach the other limbs, remembering to keep checking limbs are correctly placed.

To replace head use double string. With the aid of a small safety pin, thread the string through the neck seam of the doll's body (Figure 3.18). Someone to assist with this operation will make it much easier. Place the head in the neck opening (Figure 3.19), tightening the string while the second person holds the doll's head

15

in place. Tie 3 good knots and cut the string leaving about 5 cm (2 inches). Apply UHU glue to the string, then push one piece of string into each side of neck seam (Figure 3.20). Make sure the knot is at the back of the head.

When the UHU has completely dried, refill body and sew up the opening in the back. Your baby is now ready to dress.

Note: Surgical scissors are available at most large chemists; they are sometimes called 'surgical forceps'. Surgical scissors are a must for good elastic stringing results; they clamp shut and can be locked into several positions — a little expensive but worth every cent.

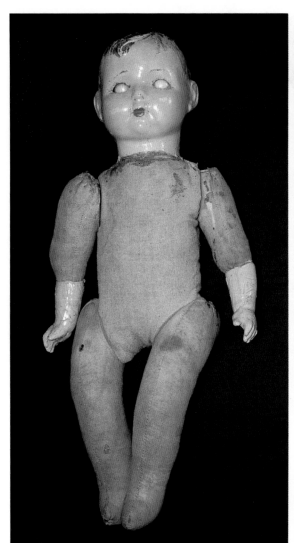

An old straw-body doll—her tin eyes seem too tired to open, her paint is cracking, hair just worn away. I couldn't change her to make her sparkling new. Could you?

Right above: Covered in biro

Right: After using Oxy-10—result after one week

Old and broken — what can we do?

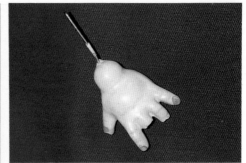

Fingers are missing

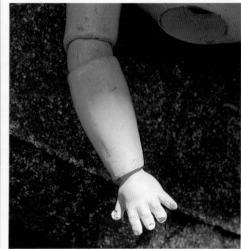

First replace them

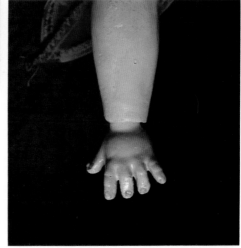

Match up the paint

4 Restoring dolls' hair and removing and fitting wigs

You will need: shampoo, conditioner, hairspray, baby oil, water mister, plastic hair brush, rubber bands, dry cleaning fluid, curling brush, hair dryer, long-nosed pliers, Aquadhere or any white wood glue

Cleaning and restoring a nylon wig

Although nylon wigs may be cleaned equally well on or off the doll's head, for the final setting and styling better results will be obtained if the wig is fixed on the doll's head.

To wash the hair, turn doll on its back, head down (Figure 4.1), and wash and condition the hair as you would your own. After the final rinsing shake doll gently but firmly to remove most of water. Keep the doll in the head down position to prevent water from running into its eyes.

Towel dry the hair. Now place a few drops of baby oil on the palm of your hand and distribute it as evenly as possible through the hair. With doll now turned onto its tummy, but still head down (Figure 4.2), brush the hair with a stiff-bristled plastic brush (inexpensive, available from most variety stores). Start from the ends of the hair, gradually working up to the roots. Brushing in this manner allows you to brush out any knots quite easily; it also prevents the loss of hair which occurs when a brush is dragged straight through it from roots to ends. The oil helps in freeing up tangles.

In no time at all the hair will be ready to set and style. You may prefer to let it dry naturally without any setting. Long hair may be suited to braids. If you decide to set the hair you can use any available hair rollers, rags or bobby pins, setting it just as you would your own.

Leave the doll in a warm airy position for at least 24 hours until the hair is bone dry; at this point we add some heat. (Heat is what holds the set in the hair and makes it semi-permanent.) Set the hair-dryer's control on hot, but be very careful — if nylon hair becomes too hot it will weld together. Too much heat can also cause burning and breakage. Holding the hair-dryer at arm's length from the doll's hair, move it constantly in a circular motion, not allowing the dryer to linger on any one section of hair. Give the hair at

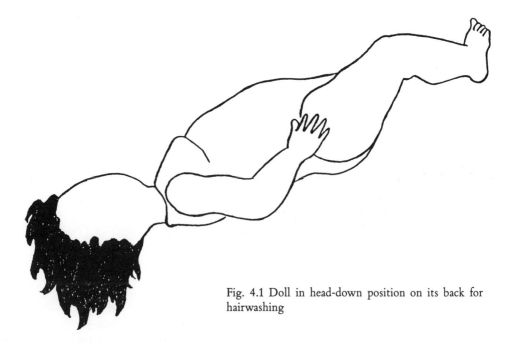

Fig. 4.1 Doll in head-down position on its back for hairwashing

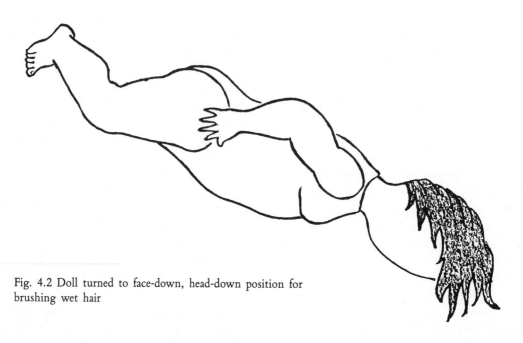

Fig. 4.2 Doll turned to face-down, head-down position for brushing wet hair

least 15 minutes to cool down before unwinding the rollers — don't be in a hurry, as hair must be unwound very carefully to avoid damage from snagging on the rollers. Using the curling brush, style the hair as you want — you may like to add ribbons or flowers.

Stand back and take a look — don't you wish your hair would shine like that?

Human hair wigs

Holding the doll in the upside down position to prevent water damage to eyes, wash and condition human hair as you would your own. Do not use any baby oil here, and only use moderate hair-dryer heat. Take great care in the washing process — if your doll has human hair it is probably very old and most likely has a cardboard pate, so do not apply much water to the scalp section.

Where a human hair wig is fixed on the doll I frequently follow the treatment described in the next section for mohair wigs. If you do decide to wash with shampoo you will need to work much faster and with more caution than if you use the mohair method, but both methods give a good result.

Set and style human hair in the same manner as nylon hair, but remember only moderate heat when drying.

Mohair wig

Using a good brand of dry cleaning fluid submerge wig briefly in a glass basin containing sufficient fluid to cover the wig. Swirl the wig about, remove from fluid and shake gently but thoroughly. If wig is fixed on the doll, protect the doll's body by covering with a plastic cape, easily made by cutting a slit in the top centre of a plastic bag. Fit the cape over the doll's head and secure with rubber bands (Figure 4.3).

Submerge hair with the doll face upward in the head-down position, and keep it in this position until the hair is almost dry, finishing drying in the open air.

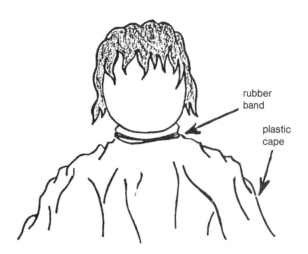

Fig. 4.3 Plastic cape protects doll's body

A windy day is great for this job, and working outside is much safer. Avoid breathing in any fumes.

If the wig is not on the doll, it can be placed in a nylon stocking after the cleaning process and hung out to dry.

To style mohair, sparingly dampen ends of hair with a fine spray of warm water, style on rollers in the usual way and spray all over with a fine mist of water.

After 24 hours dry with hot hair-dryer. Baby oil on mohair gives a very uneven and patchy result, so do not use it. When the hair is completely dry gently brush out a small section of hair at a time. Some very effective styles can be achieved with mohair; curls twisted and gently brushed around your finger look really good. This style may involve a little more time and effort but the transformation should delight you.

Fix the style with a light burst of hairspray, stand back and admire your efforts.

Removing and fitting wigs

Some old dolls have their wigs very firmly glued on, while others will lift off quite easily. I remove all wigs

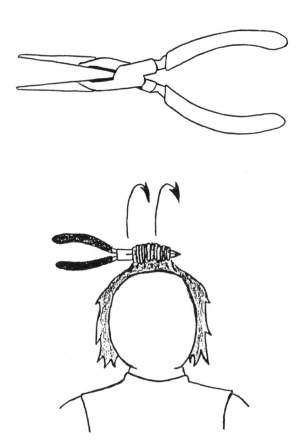

Fig. 4.4 Rolling the wig back from the doll's face using a pair of long-nosed pliers (top)

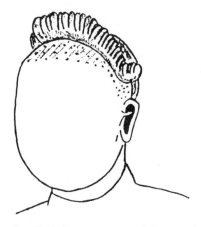

Fig. 4.5 Lift off all the outer edge of the wig first

in the same manner, using a pair of long-nosed pliers. Beginning at the front section of the hair, twist pliers around and under a small area of hair; roll the hair back around the pliers and roll towards the centre section of pate (Figure 4.4). Release, then move on to the next section of hair. It is best to slightly lift all the outer edge first (Figure 4.5), then work gradually towards the centre until the wig lifts off.

People like to keep the original wig on their doll — in the case of an old doll the wig is, of course, a big part of both the character and the monetary value of the doll. Employing the plier method of removal spares the wig a great deal of damage. It's a shame to see so many lovely old wigs vandalised by the way in which they have been removed. Of course, in some cases the wig will be so old and frail it will just break up of its own accord, but at least you will know you have done your very best to save it. Old wigs reflect a bygone era that no new wig can ever replace. All my dolls have retained their original wigs, although in some cases very little hair remains.

One easy way of maintaining an old wig while prettying up your treasure at the same time is to obtain a wig two sizes larger than the doll's head, and simply place the new wig over the original *without* the use of adhesive. This can often make the doll more attractive.

My main reason for covering an old wig is to protect and preserve it; the doll remains as close to the original as possible — after all, isn't that what caretaking a doll is all about?

Fixing a wig permanently

To fix on a new wig, cover the doll's head liberally with white glue, wiping off any excess glue that may have run down doll's face or neck. Wash off any glue that may be on your hands.

Turn the wig inside out, pushing all the hair inside (Figure 4.6). Put the front of the wig to the front of the doll's head, then roll the wig over the head,

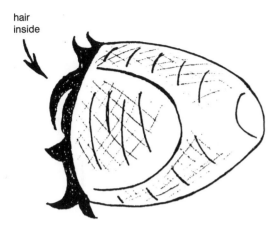

Fig. 4.6 The new wig turned inside out

hair inside

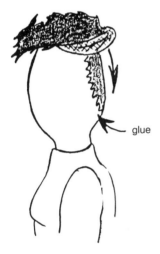

glue

Fig. 4.7 Rolling the wig over the doll's head, stretching from the outer edges

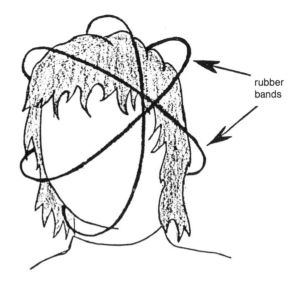

rubber bands

Fig. 4.8 Hold the wig in place with strong rubber bands while it dries

stretching from the outer edges (Figure 4.7). Check again that no glue has run onto the doll's face or neck (it's good to have a flannel on hand just in case). Place several strong rubber bands over the wig to hold it firmly in place (Figure 4.8). Allow 24 hours drying time. Remove rubber bands, brush and style hair as required.

This procedure can be a bit tricky at first, but as with everything else you do, the more wigs you fit the easier it becomes.

5 Restringing composition dolls

You will need: stringing elastic, surgical scissors, split pins, hooks, pliers. (Surgical scissors are generally available from larger chemists. They are a little expensive but looked after will last you a lifetime. Surgical scissors are a must for good stringing results.)

The first rule of restringing is to use the same gauge elastic that was originally used in the doll. In almost every case you will find, somewhere within the doll, a rusted-out piece of the first elastic — it may be in the head or hanging from one of the limbs. If there is none to be found always choose the largest and strongest elastic that will fit the stringing holes. Stringing elastic can be obtained from studios that teach reproduction porcelain dollmaking, and comes in various sizes. Studio owners are generally most helpful in advising on the correct gauge; they may also be able to assist you with wigs and eyes, even with spare parts.

Among the other essentials are a long wire hook and S-shaped hooks. My husband made my long hook (Figure 5.1) from a wire coat-hanger. The hook must be long enough to pass through the body of the doll from side to side. You may also require some S-shaped hooks (Figure 5.2); any hardware store should have these. You can make any size or shape hook you will ever need to replace missing fittings from strong florist's wire, available from hardware or florist's shops; some art

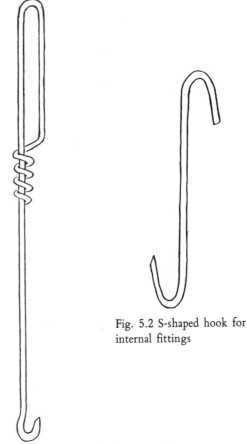

Fig. 5.2 S-shaped hook for internal fittings

Fig. 5.1 Long wire hook for restringing

suppliers also sell this kind of wire in various thicknesses. Again, my husband made most of those that I needed from old coat-hangers and other bits of wire we had. All the hooks I need to hang up my repairs for drying are all homemade too, so don't rush out spending money on items that you can quite easily make or convert from bits and pieces found in your home or around your own backyard. It's double the fun this way and much more of an achievement!

Always work on a soft surface when restringing. My preference is my large lounge. You may use a bed or get down on the carpet. It is just that I like to work on a safe roomy surface where I can lay the doll down and know that no harm will befall it.

Now with everything we need at hand let's get the doll together again.

I recommend that you always string the head and legs on the same piece of elastic; use a smaller piece of elastic to string the arms separately. This arrangement allows more flexible movement than when arms, legs and head are all attached to the one piece of elastic. First — cut a 37–38 cm (15 inch) length of elastic; place the

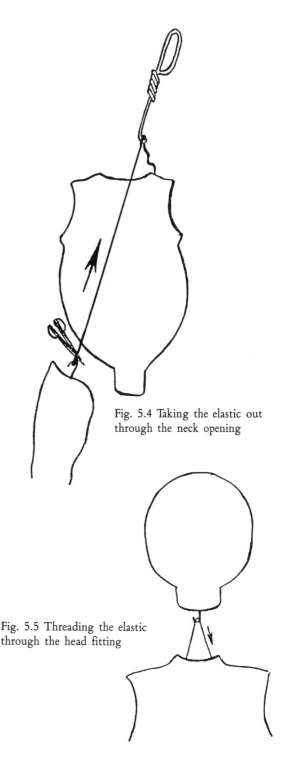

Fig. 5.4 Taking the elastic out through the neck opening

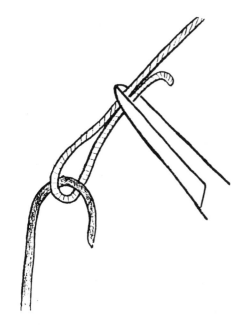

Fig. 5.3 Clamping elastic with the surgical scissors

Fig. 5.5 Threading the elastic through the head fitting

Fig. 5.6 Use the hook tool to pull elastic back through left leg body opening

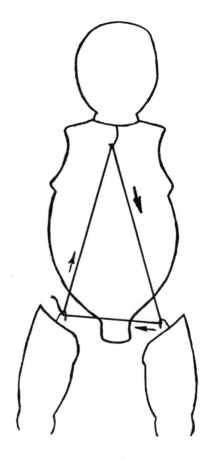

Fig. 5.7 Thread elastic through leg fitting and back through body to right leg

end through the hook or loop fitting on the right leg and pull through about 5 cm (2 inches). Clamp securely with the surgical scissors (Figure 5.3). Next, insert the long end of the elastic into right leg hole of body, taking it up through body with your hook tool. Taking the elastic out through the neck opening (Figure 5.4), thread it through the fitting in doll's head (Figure 5.5). Now push elastic back inside body and using the hook tool pull it back through left leg body opening (Figure 5.6). Thread elastic through left leg fitting, then push it through the bottom of the body to join up with right

leg (Figure 5.7). Stretching the elastic very tightly, take hold of elastic from right leg and as tightly as possible tie three good knots (Figure 5.8).

Cut off surplus elastic about 5 cm (2 inches) from knots (Figure 5.9) and release clamp. Head, body and legs should now be held tightly together (Figure 5.10).

To rethread the arms, take about 20 cm (8 inches) of elastic. Thread it through the right arm fitting and secure with clamp (Figure 5.11). Take elastic through body to left arm hole (Figure 5.12) and thread through left arm fitting. Using the hook tool pull elastic back

Fig. 5.8 Tie three good tight knots

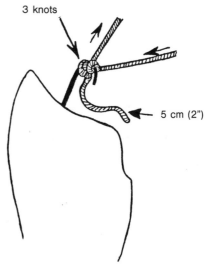

3 knots

5 cm (2")

Fig. 5.9 Cut off surplus elastic, leaving only about 5 cm (2''), and release clamp

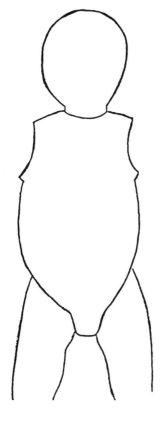

Fig. 5.10 Head, body and legs are now held tightly together

Fig. 5.11 Thread elastic through right arm fitting and clamp

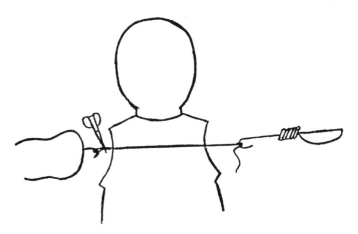

Fig. 5.12 Use hook tool to take elastic through body to left armhole

Fig. 5.13 Pull elastic back through body to right arm and tie off with three knots

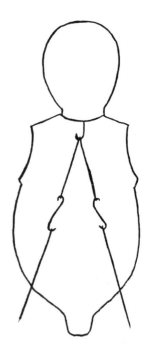

Fig. 5.15 S-shaped hooks may be used inside the bodies of large dolls

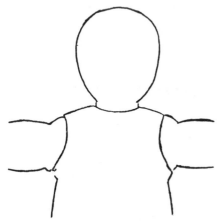

Fig. 5.14 Clamp released—arms pulled back into place

through body to right arm (Figure 5.13). Stretching tightly tie three strong knots. Cut off excess elastic and release clamp. Together again (Figure 5.14). That was an easy one, but it is the basis for all stringing.

From this you should be able to work out how to restring every possible type of doll. Double-jointed dolls may require extra wire hooks in the limbs. Sometimes you may use wire hooks inside the body (Figure 5.15).

From time to time you may have to modify the way a doll was originally strung together, especially if the fittings have corroded or broken away, when you may have to use plaster or some other heavy material to reset

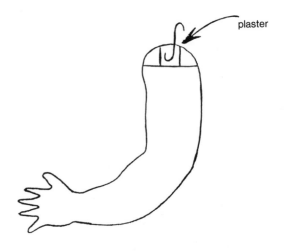

Fig. 5.16 Hook reset with plaster

fittings into the limbs (Figure 5.16). This sounds formidable, but it's not really. These little problems are bound to appear.

6 Repairing and building up composition

You will need: sawdust, Aquadhere, fine sandpaper

Composition is a mixture of one or more different compounds.

There are many different compounds for repairing composition — the one I refer to here is sawdust-based and cannot be used to repair plastic or bakelite.

You may need to replace a finger or just mend a dent — whether the job is major or minor, it can be done. This kind of mending is one of my favourite restoration jobs. There are many amazing products available to work with, among them a few I have conjured up myself and used with great success.

Let's imagine the repair we are working on is sawdust-based; our choice of material could be a sawdust mix comprising fine wood dust with white glue added. Many furniture manufacturers will allow you to collect wood dust from their workshop floor.

As wood dust is extremely fine it is advisable when collecting or mixing dust to wear a face mask that covers the nose and mouth area; this is a practice you should also employ when sanding any dry composition mixture. Protective clothing is also a good idea, not only because of the mess that you may get your clothes into, but also for health reasons, especially if your skin is sensitive to dust particles.

Mix the wood dust and glue in a deep bowl (you will use a much larger quantity of dust than glue). Gradually add glue to the dust, mixing well as you go. A wooden spoon is good for this. When you have the consistency of a soft pastry dough the mix is ready for use.

Brush some glue onto the part to be repaired, wait 5 minutes, then dampen your hands and press the amount of mixture you need into the damaged area, smoothing with your fingers as you go. Allow for some shrinkage — it's better to build up the repair a little as you can quite easily sand the excess back later on. Leave the repair to dry out for 24 hours, then using very fine sandpaper gently sand from the centre of the repair to the outer edge. Keep on sanding until with the tips of your fingers you can no longer feel where the fill was made.

Small electric sanders are available but I find I have more control and can obtain a much better finish with hand sanding. The ultimate pleasure for me is to succeed with basic tools and my own two hands.

Fingers

Faced with replacing a broken or missing finger you may think to yourself, 'I can't possibly do that', but yes, you can do it. At your first attempt you may be a little underwhelmed by the result, but if you persevere you will be able to replace a finger so well that no one will ever suspect it had been repaired.

This chapter moves from a simple filling repair to perhaps one of the hardest, a moulded finger. A finger is very tiny, with minute details, and it has to match the other fingers on the doll's hand, so naturally it is going to require more patience and expertise — remember, if at first you don't succeed...

Now seems like the perfect time to relate a little story about a little girl and her cherished doll. Some years ago an elderly lady passed on to me a beautiful old German doll; it had great sentimental value for her and she was very concerned that after she died nobody would care what became of her beloved Amelia. She showed me Amelia's hands and told me how she had been very upset as a child when several of the fingers had been broken off. She had thought it her fault the delicate fingers had broken. One day, left to amuse herself while her mother attended to the washing, she decided to make good Amelia's damaged fingers. Secretly taking a slice of fresh bread from the kitchen, she rolled and moulded it into finger shapes. She then took her mother's crochet hook and with childish hands pressed the freshly moulded fingers onto Amelia's hand. Greatly daring, she robbed an egg from the not-too-plentiful larder, using the white to glue the tiny fingers into position and coating them liberally with more egg white. Amelia was then hidden away for the new fingers to dry. Mother, on discovering one of her eggs unaccounted for, was very annoyed, and a good spanking followed for that caring little doll mother. Some 65 years later Amelia's protector confided it was worth it for dear Amelia still had all her fingers. Necessity is the mother of invention, they say. Needless to say, while ever I am Amelia's custodian her bread fingers will remain.

Fig. 6.1 Positioning of toothpick

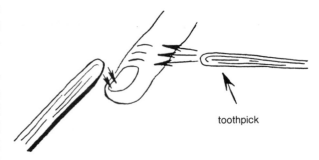

Fig. 6.2 Using toothpick to form knuckle creases and fingernails

Now let's get to that finger replacement of yours. For a framework flat wooden toothpicks are ideal as they can be bent to any required shape. Measure a piece not quite as long as the finger to be replaced, and double it, always trimming the thin end off. With a needle or similar sharp instrument bore a hole in the hand where the replacement finger will sit — it has to be deep enough and wide enough to take half the length of the cut toothpick (Figure 6.1). Put a drop of white glue into the hole. Use the wood dust mixture to mould the shape of the finger around the toothpick. Work at it until you are satisfied with the shape. If the mixture becomes too dry, moisten it with a small amount of white glue. Set the finger into the hole, pressing mix around the join to slightly overlap. Add crease marks to the finger with a needle or toothpick. Press the wide end of a toothpick onto fingertip to form nail indent (Figure 6.2).

Prop the hand into a position to allow the new repair to dry without being touched. All manner of props can be used for support — sand, plasticine, towels, books, a vice — anything that will take stress off the join will work. Make sure that once put to dry the doll will be safe from any knock or movement of any kind.

Allow a full day at least for drying. If weather is overcast, or the repair is thick, you will need a longer drying out period. Leave the doll in as airy a position as possible. If the weather is very dry and hot the repair may dry out too quickly, but any small cracks or holes appearing during this time are no cause for alarm. After sanding off, any tiny cracks can quite easily be filled using a fine brush and a dab of white glue.

When thoroughly dry and stress-tested for a firm bond, sand the finger with fine sandpaper, and paint. For the best sanding results use very small pieces of sandpaper, about 2.5 cm (1 inch) square. Sanding fingers is very intricate and time-consuming, but a good sanding is most important for a good finish. If the fingers to be sanded are not too close to each other you could try using the fine side of an emery board. Again it is what suits you and what is best suited to the repair you are working on.

Remember, always wear a mask for protection when sanding. A slightly damp towel placed under the work will tend to draw the fine dust to it — better than floating about in the air and into your lungs.

7 Repairing plaster and papier-mâché

You will need: Plasti-Bond, fine sandpaper, Aquadhere

The principles of repairing plaster and papier-mâché are basically the same as for repairing composition. We can use Plasti-Bond, papier-mâché or gesso.

Plasti-Bond

Plasti-Bond, a two-part product, functions as both filler and adhesive. Full instructions for use are on the container. Plasti-Bond is a marvellous product — it is simple and enjoyable to work with, dries quickly, is not sticky and sands off like a dream. The results will delight you. Plasti-Bond is the ultimate material for all composition restorations — but *never* for celluloid, bisque or plastics. On all other composition, if one can say a product gives 100% satisfaction then I am sure it can be said of Plasti-Bond, which can be found at most hardware stores.

Remember what I have stressed previously — the principle of trial and error. Most of the mixtures I give here can be interchanged or adapted to suit the repair at hand. If a completed wood dust repair is unsatisfactory, sand it off and try something else. Never hesitate to modify or try something entirely different.

For straight-out filling work with Plasti-Bond, use it by filling damaged area, drying and sanding. Plasti-Bond does not shrink on drying as many other products do, so you know when the filling is in and you have levelled it up that that is the end of that job. Use your fingers to smooth and level out the filling; the best time to do this is when the Plasti-Bond is almost but not quite dry, about 5 minutes after use.

The procedure for finishing is the same as set out on page 29. Only a minimum of sanding will be required; sometimes the finish is so smooth it requires no sanding at all.

To replace a finger bore a small hole in the area where finger is to be replaced (Figure 6.1, page 30), cut a wooden toothpick long enough for the finger length plus the extra bit to insert into the hand. Bend the toothpick gently to finger shape, or leave it straight — whichever style you choose make sure it is as close to the character of the original fingers as possible. Place a drop of Aquadhere into the hole in the hand, and as quickly as you can mould the Plasti-Bond around the toothpick to the correct finger shape. Carefully press the toothpick into the hole, spreading a small amount of Plasti-Bond around the join. Gently support the finger and add nail and crease marks (Figure 6.2, page 30). You must still work rapidly as such a small amount of Plasti-Bond will dry out very fast. If sanding is warranted wait a day to make sure the Aquadhere you have used in the hole is quite dry.

If a tiny crack or hole appears after completion of any composition repair, just rub a small amount of Plasti-Bond into the area — it will seal in beautifully. Also, bear in mind that painting the repair will fill up these tiny marks to a certain extent.

Aquadhere will also fill any remaining scratches or holes after painting. If you do use Aquadhere to fill a small flaw, always do so *after* sanding is completed, as Aquadhere does not sand well. It is a latex-like substance and peels when sanded. Used after sanding Aquadhere gives a good hard smooth finish; it is not waterproof, but you can quite safely spray finishing coats of paint or lacquer over it. Aquadhere can also be used as a primer or sealer before painting — two parts Aquadhere to one part water. Paint this mixture on with a soft brush, always painting in the one direction. Don't go over the surface with a second coat or you will run into trouble with peeling and air bubbles. Aquadhere is a handy product to have on your workbench as it can be used as an adhesive, sealer, filler, primer and glaze.

Papier-mâché

This recipe for papier-mâché is one I have tested and used several times, but I have to admit that after using products such as Plasti-Bond the temptation to move away from the old methods is very strong. Keep on exploring for new materials and methods, however; that's where most of the fun in doll restoration is anyway.

To make papier-mâché soak finely torn up pieces of tissue in hot water for 24 hours. Pour off the excess water, then beat until the consistency is smooth. Add Aquadhere, beating again until well blended. Use this mixture for filling or moulding. Papier-mâché does shrink a little on drying, so you may need to experiment.

Papier-mâché can also be used for model making. It makes wonderful doll's-house people and doll's-house furniture — but that's a whole new exercise. This book is about doll repairs.

Gesso

Gesso is a mixture of plaster of Paris, white glue (Aquadhere), powdered whiting and powdered zinc oxide. You can make up your own or buy it ready to use at art supply stores. I recommend the latter. If you do make your own make up a small quantity, as like papier-mâché it has a short life unless you add a preservative such as 4% formalin solution.

Gesso is used like paint, and is irreplaceable for repairing the cardboard bodies of old double-jointed dolls. It is applied with a good soft brush, stroking in the one direction. Build up as many coats as required, drying out between coats. Here again the good old fingers come into use, smoothing out the final application. If sanding is required, always sand in the one direction. Gesso can also be used as a filler for small holes or flaws.

Before painting over gesso prime with 2 parts Aquadhere, 1 part water formula; this prevents the paint being swallowed up by the powder materials in the gesso.

8 Bisque repairs

You will need: kaolin powder, Selleys Porcelain Repair Kit

Bisque repair is the most exacting of all repair work. Nevertheless it's well worth the effort of mastering all its aspects as the satisfaction is so much greater when you challenge yourself.

You may sometimes sigh at the sight of a doll in such a sorry state that for a fleeting moment you think it is beyond help. But if you're like me you won't be able to resist that doll, no matter how bad the injuries. There will be times when it will seem an impossible task to even know where to begin.

But picture in your mind how the doll will look when you achieve the impossible and bring back that lost charm and beauty — surely it has to be worth at least a try. Don't abandon that heritage.

The kaolin mixture used here is one that I have used many times. (There are many more, some of which I have had to concoct out of necessity for a particular repair.) This is a good basic mix which dries as hard as bisque and does not require firing. Painting and finishing differ from the method used on composition.

Small bags of kaolin are available from art shops that sell materials used in pottery crafts. It's not expensive. Selleys Porcelain Repair Kit is similar to Araldite, except that it is greyish-white, not clear. It's not always available

locally, so I suggest you ring Selleys to find your closest distributor.

On a clean tile or old plate place equal portions of porcelain glue and kaolin. Gradually work in small quantities of kaolin, using an old knife. Blend well into a solid dough and knead with fingers until well combined and the mixture is firm but pliable. Spread a little porcelain glue on the base of the repair, then press the mixture into or around the repair.

The kaolin mix usually begins to dry in about an hour, depending on climatic conditions. It is important not to hurry the drying out period with added heat as throughout the first part of the drying time you must constantly monitor the repair for imperfections. This is where those indispensable fingers come into their own once again. Being of the old school I do not encourage the use of any machine or gadget when hands and fingers can feel and do so much better — a repair done by hand is no longer just a repair, it is part of you. I think it is one of the faults of today's society — we have left behind our ability to do for ourselves. Australia's Aboriginal artists and sculptors couldn't run to the store to buy paints, brushes, canvases or tools — and just look at their glorious creations.

If using hands and fingers is not for you, that's fine — there are any amount of little machines with motors

Start with right leg with elastic in place using a split pin instead of knots to secure elastic

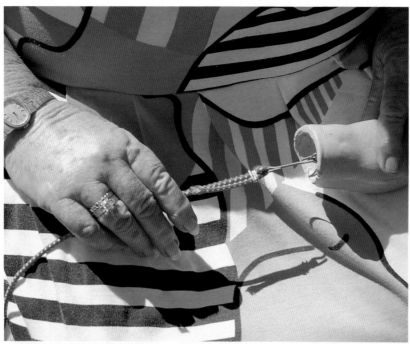

Below left: Thread elastic up through leg
Centre: Thread elastic up through body and pass it through the hook on the neck
Right: Take elastic down through body and secure with clamp

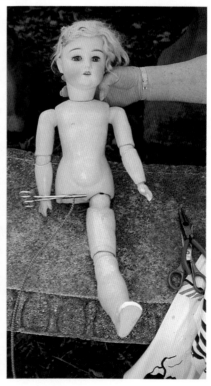

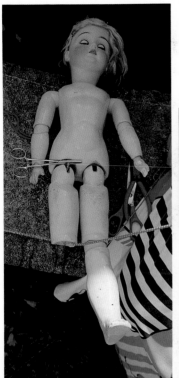

Thread elastic through upper leg

Secure with split pin

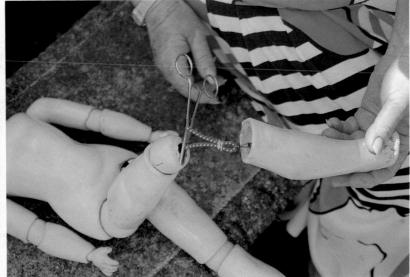

Together again

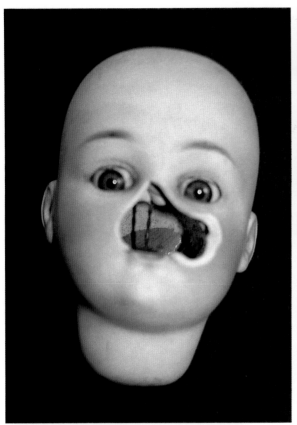

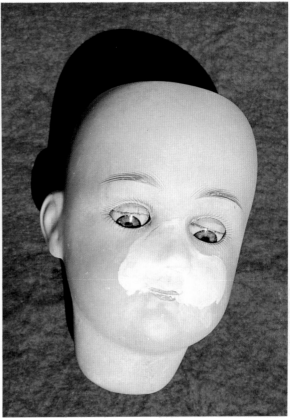

Above left: This bisque head needed quite a lot of rebuilding

Above: Using the method for replacing a celluloid nose (page 47), the damaged area was built up and moulded. The material used was kaolin and porcelain adhesive (page 34)

A felt doll of the type made during the war years when dolls were hard to come by. This one, made in 1942, has been brightened up with some TLC

The techniques of doll repair can be applied elsewhere ... a severely damaged plaster statue in the process of restoration using Aquadhere, plaster of Paris and gesso

Below left: A doll in need of restoration
Below right: The same doll after being cleaned and polished. Sporting a new wig and new clothes, she is ready to charm again

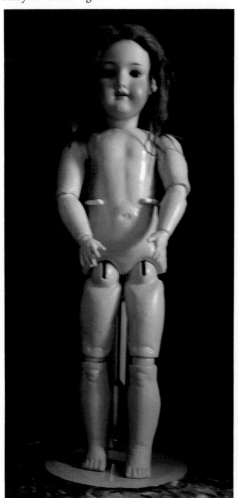

that you can spend your money on, but I can't help you with stockists.

Now getting back to our kaolin repair — if any flaws do appear during drying out slightly dampen your finger with a little water and gently smooth them away, working from the centre to the outer edge of the repair. Remember, as in other fillings and with rebuilding work, to slightly overlap the repair area.

Finger repairs are made in the same manner as with composition (page 29). Remember to maintain your scrutiny for imperfections. If any appear get to work with a slightly dampened finger and gently smooth away. Surveillance should continue for at least 4 hours. After this the repair should be propped at a safe angle for drying.

If a small piece of the doll has completely broken away, you will have to use cold moulding wax (available at most art stores) as a base for the repair. Unlike other wax cold moulding wax does not need to be melted, just kneaded by hand until it becomes soft and manageable. You must be able to gain access to the inside of the doll's head to use this technique. Mould the wax to fit directly over the missing area, pressed up hard against the surrounding area (Figure 8.1). The wax

should be at least 1.5 (½ inch) thick. If the wax does not stick to the bisque sufficiently place a strip of masking tape or other suitable adhesive tape behind the wax and onto the bisque (Figure 8.2). Use your fingers or the back of a teaspoon to smooth and smooth the wax to the right shape.

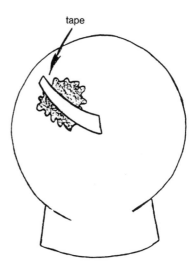

Fig. 8.2 Holding the wax to the head with masking tape

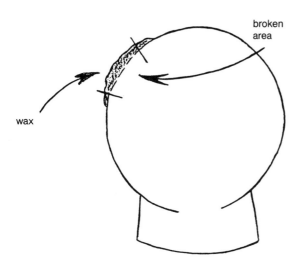

Fig. 8.1 Wax moulded over missing area

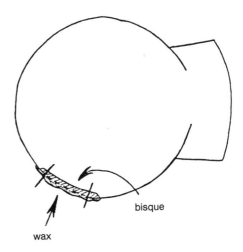

Fig. 8.3 The kaolin mix is pressed against the wax from inside the head

Bisque is very delicate and exacting work. It's very important that all joins to be repaired are thoroughly cleaned before any restoration is attempted. Scrub the broken edges of the porcelain in warm soapy water, using a small brush. Allow to dry completely, then wipe with methylated spirits, using a piece of clean fabric (silk if possible, as it will not leave lint or fluff behind.

Prepare the kaolin mix, this time modifying it to a softer texture. Spread porcelain glue on edges of join, then add the kaolin mix to the wax support, smoothing out mixture and pressing firmly to the edges (Figure 8.3).

This type of repair will take a lot longer. If you do a good smoothing job while kaolin repairs are drying there should be no need to sand as the kaolin mixture drys beautifully smooth. If you do need to sand, use a fine wet and dry sandpaper. When working with epoxy resins such as Araldite or porcelain adhesives, keep tools clean by dipping them in methylated spirits as soon as you have used them — this prevents resins from sticking.

Sometimes it becomes necessary to make a plaster mould for a missing part; this kind of job is far too complicated to cover in a book dealing with repairs, as casting and mould making call for an extensive programme of learning. There are many helpful books available on the subject, or you can enrol in a mould making course, which I found very valuable. If you have a yen to try your hand at making your very own, one and only doll, then take the class. Had I just wanted to learn for the sake of doing repairs I would have worked out my own system, as I often did before I took the course.

Briefly I will outline a basic method that may help you to go on for yourself. When a piece is missing it is possible to make a mould of the missing part using cold moulding wax. This is simple if you have a flair for modelling but a good bit harder if you don't. The general idea is that you make a cast of an identical piece to replace the missing part you wish to repair, then using the compound best suited to the repair you fill the wax mould. When the compound is dry you remove the

wax, then sand and fit the new piece into the repair area with the use of a suitable adhesive. I hope this little piece of general information may tempt you to put on your thinking cap and go about some experimenting of your own. There are many techniques; some require more patience than others but all are worth persisting with.

The kaolin method is the simplest method of repairing bisque, but many other exciting materials are available. Don't be afraid to try things out — I am sure some

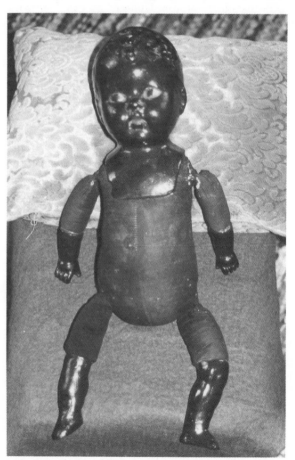

This doll's missing right leg was replaced with a leg modelled from Barbola (page 41). One of my very first repairs, it now seems pretty ghastly. Sometimes I think I will redo it—but then it would not be my first hand-moulded leg, would it?

of your discoveries will astound you. Over the years I have repaired countless pieces of crockery, vases and ornaments using the kaolin method. One old Wedgwood serving dish survived for many years, even being submitted to the test of a hot oven. The dish wasn't painted after the repair as the dried kaolin mixture happened to be the same colour as the dish. The mend never looked out of place and served us well. As you gain more experience so your confidence will grow; there will be no repair you will feel apprehensive about tackling.

The products listed below all give great results for bisque work as well, and are all well worth trying out. The first two are suitable for casting missing pieces.

Arbee cold moulding

Arbee is a cold moulding latex somewhat like a balloon when dry. It's very flexible, great for moulding fingers and hands. Instructions are on the tin.

Rubber casting resin

This product has to be melted down before use. It offers excellent results and will come off difficult undercuts without any problem. It's a bit smelly during melting, and you have to be very careful as it's flammable, as of course most of these materials are. This one should be treated with extra care as it is in close contact with heat.

Plaster compound

A very old mixture, surely one that was used by our grandparents. Mix plaster of Paris with an equal quantity of powdered gelatin, add hot water and blend well.

Porcelain filler

Available from hardware or some bathroom furniture suppliers. There are several brands, generally used for repair work to broken or chipped tiles or bathroom fittings.

Barbola

Barbola is excellent, a pliable, ready-mixed compound available at most art and craft shops.

Acrylic dental filler

A trip to a dental supplier will be needed for this one. It's suitable only for very small work. It does not shrink, but is quite expensive.

Paper clay

This is a new product on the market, made by a Japanese company. It's a self hardening compound that dries like fired clay. I have not used it yet but it seems very interesting from the literature. See index for details of availability.

There are many other proprietary lines available and it's a never-ending process of discovery, testing out new-found products.

9 Pedigree and Cherub repairs

You will need: Vertex SC (self-curing compound), spatula, flat wooden toothpicks, glass egg-cup, eye-bath or similar small container

Vertex is a two-part mix of powder and liquid hardener only available at dental suppliers. Although initially Vertex is a little costly to buy it does last a very long time. If you intend doing a lot of repairs to these types of dolls you will most likely have to buy more liquid hardener before the powder runs out. Vertex comes in a white powder, which dries to a cloudy white, and is also available in a pinkish colour. A combination of the white and pink will often give you the exact colour you require for Pedigree type dolls. Mostly I stay with the white for light yellowish coloured dolls.

The results I have achieved with Vertex on heavy plastic or bakelite compositions are by far the best I've had. Vertex dries very fast so you will need a bit of practice on an old spare part before beginning on repairs. It can be used for filling, repairing cracks and holes, and modelling fingers. It adheres to the base material and dries as hard as a rock.

Vertex is used in a slightly different manner to the mixtures we have so far used. The area to be treated should always be first sanded with a medium sandpaper to reduce its smooth shiny texture and guarantee secure bonding with the Vertex. For mixing use a small glass container about the size of an egg-cup (it *must* be glass). Due to Vertex's rapid-drying quality only mix a small amount each time. You will also need a spatula or a very fine narrow knife with a flexible blade, and flat wooden toothpicks which are good for mixing or filling really small cracks or holes.

When you are ready to start work, pour a few drops of hardener into the container, add a tiny amount of powder and stir with spatula or toothpick to a firm consistency. Quickly smear a meagre drop of the liquid onto the area to be repaired, then quickly apply mixed Vertex to the repair area. As the Vertex comes in contact with the extra liquid applied to the base of the mend it will break down to a softer consistency. If it begins drying out before you have time to complete the repair it can be slowed down by smearing a dab more liquid onto the mixture.

As Vertex dries so hard, sanding is arduous, so when you are satisfied with the repair with a smear of liquid on your finger quickly run your finger over the repair and smooth it over. You may have to do this more than once as the liquid dries out fast. But — be very careful adding liquid to the finished repair as too much will dissolve the repair completely! Does that sound frightening? I sincerely hope not, as Vertex is one of the easiest products I have ever worked with.

To replace a finger, use a needle to melt a hole into

the replacement area of sufficient size to take a toothpick and add a tiny drop of liquid hardener into the hole. Cut a toothpick to the length of the finger, allowing extra to insert into hole, and bend to required shape. Dip toothpick into firm Vertex mixture, twirl it around, quickly shape and insert into hole. Set about any final smoothing and marking of nail and finger creases *with all speed.*

Another method is to dip toothpick into Vertex mixture, taking up only a thin coating, then insert into finger hole. Allow to dry, then with a small cheap brush quickly paint over finger with more mixture until you have the required size. Smooth out and add markings.

You will always have to work as if the devil were behind you when working with Vertex — this is why I suggest you play around with the method before you attempt the real thing. Also, this is one mix you use your fingers with as little as possible, as it clings and dries so fast. Don't be put off using Vertex, it really is excellent; it may take a bit longer to adjust to than some other products, but really there are no problems that cannot be rectified by just adding extra liquid to the repair. The liquid will dissolve the mend completely, so just wipe it away and start again.

10 Repairing celluloid dolls

You will need: Selleys 5-Minute Araldite, kettle with spout, sandpaper, toothpick, soft cardboard, needle, thread, adhesive tape (not all required for every job)

Celluloid is a very old material. Any doll made from this delicate composition is well worth saving. As far as I am aware celluloid is no longer manufactured to the same formula as that originally used for these distinctive old dolls. Celluloid dolls have a beauty all of their own, but unfortunately because of their fragile nature many have been lost down through the years. The owners of these easily damaged dolls had to handle them with extra care. Their main injuries were dents, although another reason for their early demise was fire — celluloid is highly flammable and I am told many dolls were lost to their loving owners by the unforgivable pranks of brothers and friends. Many dolls that were sat too close to the fire also just melted away. What a heart-breaking trauma for a little girl to have to endure.

Not only is celluloid very fragile to handle — you must also be very cautious with your choice of glues and other substances for repair work. Some adhesives will soften or even dissolve the celluloid — disaster! Always test new products on old parts that are damaged beyond repair, and *always* keep doll away from all heat, especially from anyone holding a cigarette.

To remove dents from celluloid, boil a kettle until steam is coming out of the spout in a steady strea. Turn the heat down, maintaining steam flow, and suspend the dented area over the steam. The dent may pop out immediately or it may take some time. Dents in the head section can sometimes be reached from inside. If this is possible it will help to release the dent more quickly if you can push a pencil with an eraser on the end inside and using soft pressure work the eraser behind the dent. Unfortunately it is not always possible to get inside.

Dents are unpredictable; if there is any crushing or cracking of the repair area, the job can often be tedious as celluloid appears to have a memory! Some dents, after being completely removed, show a tendency to sink back after a day or two. While a second steam treatment is in progress gentle pressure around the dent will often help it pop. As soon as the dent has released place the part under cold running water for a minute or so with the repair facing down. This treatment will help prevent the dent reappearing. If it does come back again repeat the treatment, allowing a longer time under the water after the dent has popped.

The safest adhesive for celluloid repairs is Selleys 5-Minute Araldite. Using the 5-minute drying adhesive means the repair can be carried out quickly without risk to the celluloid from a solvent remaining wet and active. If necessary the repair can be held in the hand for the short drying time. This can sometimes be very helpful when trying to effect a flush join on brittle material.

As you become more adept on the doll repair trail you will overcome many obstacles along the way, including devising ingenious little ways of supporting repairs while they are drying. Sand is one of the best props as the repair can be laid down at any angle for support. Wire structures and plasticine are both good, too. Each repair job differs in the way it has to be balanced, just one of the tiny problems that you will solve when it confronts you.

Cracks or splits at the joins are very common on celluloid dolls, but they are relatively simple, straightforward repair jobs. All that is required is Araldite, toothpick and sandpaper. With fine sandpaper rough up the celluloid at the repair area. Mix the 2-part Araldite on a clean tile; with a toothpick and a steady hand take up a small amount of mixture on the flat end of toothpick and quickly run the adhesive down the crack (Figure 10.1). Wipe off any excess with a clean rag. Move the repaired area backwards and forwards, watching that adhesive does not run to one section — it must stay evenly distributed. When there is no movement in the adhesive, press down on it slightly to flatten it onto the surface of the repair.

Although the Araldite dries a faintly different colour to the celluloid, if the repair is done correctly it never looks out of place and blends in amazingly well. As for durability, I have seen some pretty rough treatment meted out to dolls that have been repaired by this method and they just keep holding up. Hard as it may be to believe, some folk actually give children these old dolls to play with. I'm all for children experiencing the pleasure of owning old dolls but before this happens they should be taught to appreciate the unique value of such an heirloom.

Fixing joins that have split open may require extra pressure to bring them back together. After completing such a join secure it in the exact position with strips

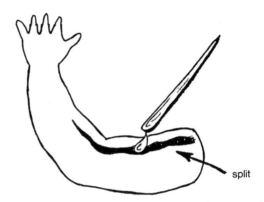

Fig. 10.1 Using a toothpick to apply Araldite to a split

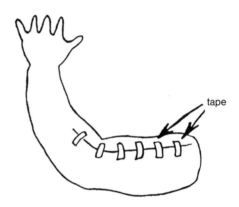

Fig. 10.2 Adhesive tape used to hold a mend together until dry

of adhesive tape pulled tightly across the join (Figure 10.2). A good-looking repair is no good at all if it has no strength.

Another common repair to a celluloid doll is to replace a missing nose. (Was it bitten off? Did dear brother cut it off? This we may never know.) A new nose takes a bit more effort but you will be delighted with the result; nothing looks much worse than a doll with half a nose unless, of course, it's a doll with no nose at all, so of course you are going to completely rebuild that nose.

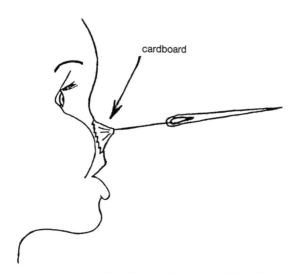

cardboard

Fig. 10.3 Using a thread to position the cardboard

I know you will initially feel reluctant about this, so you should experiment once again on any old unsalvageable piece. Any repair you feel apprehensive about you should of course try out first using old pieces of plaster, bisque or whatever the material may be until you master the technique.

Now for the nose: cut out a small piece of soft cardboard, slightly larger than the hole in the doll's nose. Select a colour as near as possible to the celluloid; a shade darker will be fine. Place the cardboard inside the nose, allowing it to roughly take up the shape of the nose. Once you are sure that the size of cardboard is right thread a fine needle with thread a similar colour to the cardboard, tie a good strong knot at the end, and draw it through the centre of the cardboard (Figure 10.3). Cut thread off the needle, leaving about 15 cm (6 inches) of thread attached to the cardboard. Refit cardboard into the doll's nose, bringing it to the general shape of the nose. The cardboard should be sitting in the hole and hard up against the celluloid, with no gaps around the edges. Using the thread pull and manoeuvre the cardboard until you are satisfied with the basic shape.

Mix Araldite, take up thread and pull as tightly as possible. Holding thread with one hand, begin covering cardboard shape with Araldite, continuing filling until you reach outer joins. Allow some Araldite to overlap the edge of the repair. While the Araldite is setting move doll to and fro to ensure mixture is remaining in repair area. When the Araldite is almost dry to touch gradually mould with fingers to ensure a perfect shape. Cut thread as close to new nose as possible, then gently smooth over with fingers where thread was cut; not only will the thread be invisible, it will also be almost impossible to detect that the nose has been replaced. In fact people who are not aware will never notice any difference.

The more nose surgery you carry out the more skilful you will become. Unfortunately there will always be people who when you point out the repair to them will remark, 'Oh yes, I noticed it immediately.' (I guess you know one or two also.) These people are the self-confessed experts — whatever you do never take any notice of them or allow them to discourage you in any way.

Earlier in the book I said that in some cases you will be able to transform a broken doll back to its original beauty. I will go even further now and say, sometimes to even better than the original, as many old dolls were very poorly made, the mould line left unsanded, painting in some cases horrific. Many were turned out on assembly lines and just not given that personal finishing touch, the touch that you are going to add.

The technique for replacing celluloid fingers is the same as for repairing the nose. This process also applies to bisque or composition repairs of this nature. Every repair you perform can be varied to suit other materials; the method remains, only the use of materials is different. If you were mending a similar repair on composition you would of course use wood dust or Plasti-Bond; for Pedigree-type repairs you would use Vertex compound. As I remarked earlier, it's basically common sense.

Amelia—her hands lovingly replaced by a child using bread dough and egg white (page 30)

Below left: This old French doll came to me in her original muslin dress, her mohair wig in excellent condition. New clothes cover the old, but there was still a magic about that old muslin dress. The slight cross in her eyes adds individuality

Below right: This celluloid doll had severe denting on face and body. The steaming method of restoration (page 44) was successful, althoug it had to be repeated several times in some areas where there were deep depressions and some crushing

This baby doll, not valuable as far as dollars go, but dearly loved by one little girl, came to me with one eye shut, one eye open, hair a tangled disaster. Now she is ready to be worn out with love again

Below left: Just plastic, you may say, but somebody's favourite
Right: Ready to go home

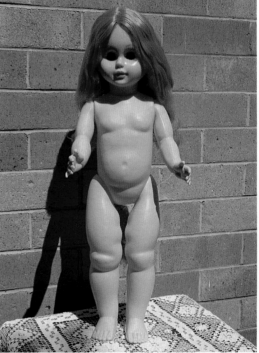

11 Restringing celluloid dolls

You will need: stringing elastic, 2.5 cm (1 inch) split pins, surgical scissors, small pliers, florist's wire

One of the problems with beautiful old celluloid dolls is the splitting and cracking of joins over the years. For this reason I recommend using medium gauge stringing elastic rather than the heavy elastic that may have been used originally, as the latter places too much stress on the old celluloid.

Cut a length of elastic to pass twice through the body of the doll. About 2.5 cm (1 inch) from one end tie one good tight knot (Figure 11.1). Open split pin, twist once around elastic directly behind knot, and press tightly shut with small pliers (Figure 11.2). Leave the two ends of the split pin facing out in opposite directions (Figure 11.3). Push the knotted end of elastic and the pin into the hole of right leg (Figure 11.4). If it is difficult to push the pin through the hole trim a little off each end with the pliers (a gentle twist back and forth will

do the trick). When the pin is inside the leg it will be impossible to remove it — once the stretch of the elastic is applied it will never come out of its own accord.

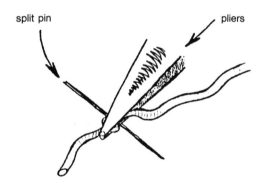

Fig. 11.2 Press split pin shut with pliers

Fig. 11.1 Tie a knot 2.5 cm (1'') from the end of the elastic

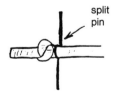

Fig. 11.3 The ends of the split pin are opened out 180°

49

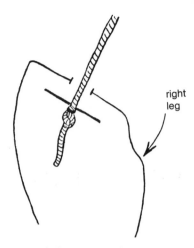

right
leg

Fig. 11.4 Split pin and elastic inserted into leg

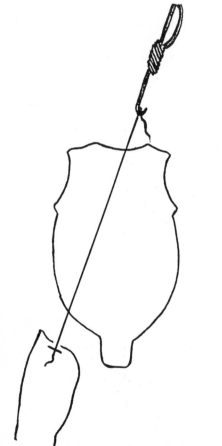

Fig. 11.5 Elastic threaded from right leg to head

Fig. 11.6 Elastic threaded through head fitting

Fig. 11.7 Take the elastic back down through body to left leg opening

Next, thread elastic into right leg body hole up through body (Figure 11.5), then out through neck opening. Run the elastic through the wire hook or loop hanging from the doll's head (Figure 11.6), then pass it back down through the body to come out through the left leg body hole (Figure 11.7).

To make this task easier twist some fine florist's wire around the end of the elastic and back about 15 cm (6 inches)(Figure 11.8). This support allows you more control in guiding the elastic through the bottom hole.

Pull the elastic out of the left leg hole (Figure 11.9) and remove the wire. Stretch the elastic very tightly. This part of the operation is very important, as the elastic has to be very tight — there must be no slack whatever. Now secure elastic with clamp. About 7–8 cm (3 inches) from the clamp tie a good knot, pulling tight as before. Fix a split pin as for the other leg and cut off spare elastic to leave about 2.5 cm (1 inch). Insert split pin into left leg hole and release clamp (Figure 11.10).

For arms cut off about 20 cm (8 inches) of elastic. Proceed as for right leg — tie knot, fix split pin into arm hole, twist wire around end of elastic, insert through right body arm hole to opposite arm hole, push through hole, remove wire, stretch tight and secure with clamp. About 7–8 cm (3 inches) along elastic tie a good knot, fix split pin, cut off elastic 2.5 cm (1 inch) past knot, insert into left arm hole, release clamp.

Together again. Now wasn't that easy, or were you all fingers and thumbs? Next time will be so much easier. The photographs on the next page may help.

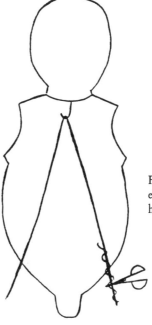

Fig. 11.9 Pull the wired elastic through left leg hole and remove wire

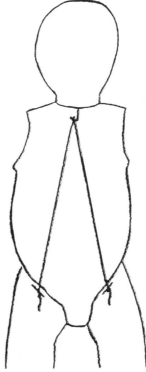

Fig. 11.10 Push split pin into left leg hole and remove clamp

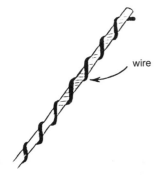

wire

Fig. 11.8 Florist's wire twisted around the elastic

Restringing celluloid in photographs

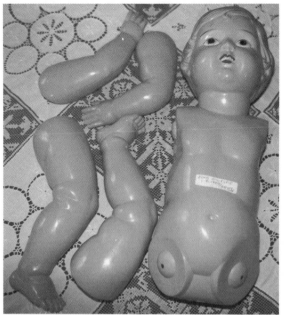

In pieces now, but otherwise in very good condition

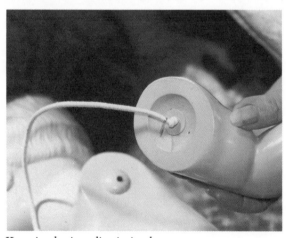

Knot in elastic, split pin in place

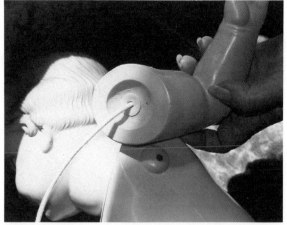

Knot and split pin pressed into arm opening

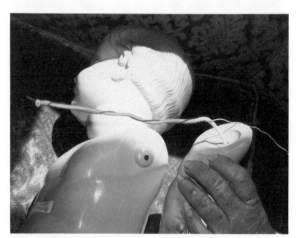

Wire twisted around elastic to help guide elastic through body to right side

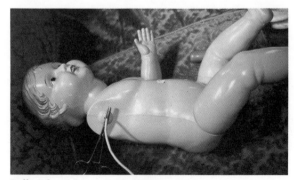

Pull tight, secure with clamp

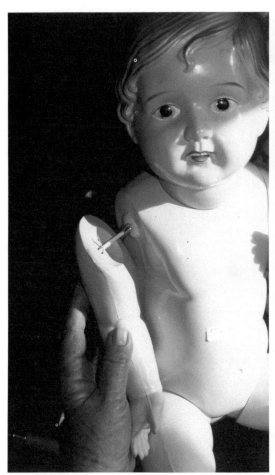

Knot elastic, position split pin, insert into right arm, release clamp

A good polish with magic oil finishes the job

12 Painting

You will need: acrylic paints, oil paints, brushes, bamboo skewers, Duncan's paint, Duncan's matt finish spray, Mayco bisque stains

Painting composition

All my painting is done by hand using quality sable brushes and fine bamboo skewers for lips, eye outlines, eyebrows, nostrils and any other fine stroke work, a method taught to me years ago by a wonderful old Sister of Mercy, whose maxim was, 'the hand that holds the brush has the ultimate control.'

As important as the hand that holds the brush are the hand that mixes the colour and the eye that knows when the colour is right. When repainting or touching up a repair the colour match has to be perfect. Near enough is never good enough and when it comes to matching colour it's more important than ever. When repainting an area overlap the repair a little to allow for better blending.

Never repaint the whole doll just to get the colour right, but always maintain as much of a doll's originality as possible, whether repairing or repainting.

Before starting to paint test and test again to ensure the colour is right. As paint dries the colour changes slightly, so when testing always allow the paint to dry out. When the colour is right to your eye test for a perfect match on an unobtrusive area of the doll; the bottom of a foot is ideal. Paint on the mix and allow it to dry; if the colour is not suitable wipe it off with a damp cloth and wipe dry. No damage will be done as you are working with water-based paint. Try again until the colour matches.

You will need tubes of acrylic paint in white, red, yellow, blue, brown; a good quality brush (these are available at art stores); bamboo skewers (most supermarkets); you will also need Duncan's flesh colour waterpaint, and for sealing and finishing Duncan's matte finish sealer (these last two are available from ceramic or reproduction porcelain doll studios), a spatula or flat stick for mixing paint, some old dishes or plastic throwaway containers, a few small jars (the ones that tablets come in are very handy — if you make a mix that is not suitable for one doll it may be the exact colour for another, so store it for another day).

Starting with the flesh colour waterpaint, add extra colours to work up the desired shade. You may need to add a touch of red for a pinkish skin, a touch of yellow for another, a dab of brown for yet another, a touch of white if the tone is too dark. Always work adding just one or two drops of the extra colour.

When you are happy with the colour paint the area for repair, adding a few drops of water if the paint seems a little thick. A thin coat is much better than a thick coat. While the paint is still wet (about half dry is best), smooth over very lightly with your fingers for a better blend. Allow to dry out. This time will vary from a couple of minutes to an hour.

One coat of paint is never enough. You may need 5 or 6 coats for a good finish — the number cannot be specified, but you will know when a good depth of colour is reached.

When painting blush areas such as cheeks always blend in the cheek colour before the last coat of base colour is dry. With the tips of your fingers begin blending from the centre of the cheeks, working out towards ears then lifting fingers upwards. This is very precise and requires a certain amount of practice — any old doll is suitable for practice purposes.

You will need to practice the eye and lip technique for all fine work such as eyelashes, eyebrows and eye outlines. My work is done with bamboo skewers. They have a very fine point on one end, and are used in the same manner as a fine brush. Once you master the use of the stick I don't think you will ever return to the brush for delicate work; it may be initially frustrating but persistence is the key.

If you have a composition doll whose paintwork has crazed take some matching colour paint into the palm of your hand and rub it vigorously into the crazed area. This method of restoring crazing is more successful than brushing paint on. If you have the correct colour the result will be perfect.

Bear in mind you can't do any damage when you are working with water-based paints. This is the reason for beginning with acrylics — it's the most sensible way to learn. When you are satisfied with the work you are doing it is time to advance to oils.

Painting bisque

There are two methods for painting bisque — oils and Mayco bisque stains. My preferred method is painting with oils — they are glorious to work with. They do take quite a time to dry, which in many respects is good as you have longer to make sure no blemishes remain. Blending work is so much easier as the paint is not drying out under your fingers as it does with acrylics. Faces painted in oil look more alive, with a translucent quality about them.

If you have to paint eyes, on any doll, always paint the white of the eye first. When the white is dry paint in the iris, and then the pupil. If one eye is still good use that for your guide. Usually, even when both eyes need attention, there is enough paint left somewhere to use as a colour guide. If only part of the eye is damaged, after repair only paint the built-up area that paint is missing from. Do not repaint the entire eye.

Always add a fine white dot or flash to the finished iris — this adds sparkle and life to the doll's eye. I have seen some bisque dolls' eyes beautifully restored except that the white flash has been omitted — I can never work out why.

The majority of bisque dolls having sleeping eyes so you may never have to face repainting their eyes, nevertheless you will be called upon to paint many others.

The main use of oils on bisque is for face painting and touching up repaired areas. Colours are mixed just as they are for acrylics, except you will not use water at any stage. Follow the principles outlined on page 54. When restoration is completed spray the area with one of the Duncan sealers or finish with a polish of baby oil.

The second method of bisque painting uses Mayco bisque stains. These come in dozens of different colours, from flesh shades to reds for lips, blues for eyes and many shades of brown. These stains do a very good job but I recommend you gather a lot of experience before trying to work with them. Mayco stains dry quickly so you have very little chance of blending them, and they do not intermix well. They are excellent if you obtain the wanted colour straight off the shelf. They do require a lot of work to remove them if you make an error in application. This does not mean you should avoid them, but do take care.

Painting celluloid and Pedigree-type dolls

Celluloid dolls are painted with acrylics, following the principles on page 54, but allow a good hour's drying time between coats. When painting is finished apply a single coat of clear nail hardener to the eyes and lips. This seals the paint and gives an enduring finish.

Celluloid cheeks can only be painted with oil, however.

Pedigree types and celluloid dolls should be finished with a light coat of the magic baby oil, but *always* do any painting *before* oiling. The oiling is the final beauty treatment.

Repainting whole dolls

For composition and bisque dolls that have to be repainted completely I have found Duncan's matt finish spray to give the best result. (It can also be used on small areas by spraying a small amount into a clean glass container, painting it onto repair area and very quickly smoothing over with a finger. The application can be repeated until the desired effect is reached.)

Many old composition dolls were painted and glazed by the dipping method. This provides a truly lovely finish, but is not practicable unless you intend dipping several dolls at once.

A handy drying frame can be made from a wire coathanger (Figure 12.1). All drying should be done in a dust-free, airy position sheltered from direct sunlight.

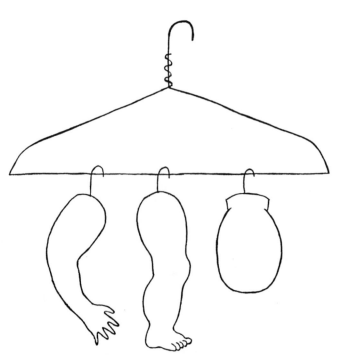

Fig. 12.1 A wire coathanger makes a handy drying frame

13 Resetting sleeping eyes

You will need: plaster of Paris, Vaseline, Blu-tack

Many old dolls have blown glass eyes which are not only quite valuable but also very fragile. Take very great care when working with these eyes. It is a good idea to have a sheet of foam on the workbench on which to lay them down safely.

Before doing anything with the eyes, familiarise yourself with the way they sit in the doll's head. Take special note of the position of the old plaster that originally held the eyes. Usually there will be a clearly visible age mark surrounding this area, enabling you to replace the plaster in exactly the right position. Make sure the inside of the doll's head is clean and free of dust.

The next step is to protect the eyes with Vaseline. The Vaseline forms a barrier between the plaster and the eyes, preventing the plaster from making contact with the eyes. As we require the eyes to open and shut we have to have a barrier that the plaster cannot adhere to, otherwise the eyes won't move! If no Vaseline is at hand you can substitute oil, detergent or soft soap. Using a small brush apply the Vaseline to the back and sides of eyes; also brush a smear over the front section of the eyes (Figure 13.1). This is a precautionary measure in the event of any plaster seeping through.

Place a piece of Blu-tack the size of a pea at the front between the eyes (Figure 13.2). Put the eyes aside. Pour

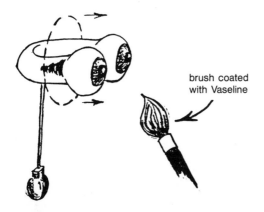

brush coated
with Vaseline

Fig. 13.1 Apply Vaseline to the back and sides of the eyes, and to the front

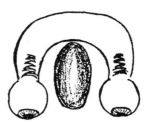

Fig. 13.2 Position a piece of Blu-tack between the eyes at the front

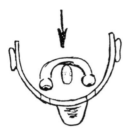

Fig. 13.3 Press eyes into position in head

Figure 13.4 Check that eyes are sitting correctly in the doll's head

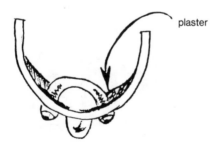

Fig. 13.5 Allow an overlap of plaster of Paris to come slightly behind the eyes

about 40 ml (2 tablespoons) of water into a small container, gradually adding a small quantity of plaster. Stir and continue adding plaster until it reaches the consistency of very thick batter. The mixture should peak, not droop. Press eyes into position in doll's head with the Blu-tack (Figure 13.3), being careful not to touch any part of the eyes coated with Vaseline. Lift the doll's head above your own and check that eyes are sitting correctly (Figure 13.4). Set head down. Using a small spoon drop plaster onto each side of eyes and inside wall of head where old plaster was. Allow an overlap of plaster to come slightly behind the sides of eyes (Figure 13.5) — this will prevent the eyes falling back into the doll's head when laid on her back.

Check again that eyes are placed correctly by carefully lifting head over your head once more. Set head face down in a safe place until the plaster is set hard. Setting time can vary from one hour to 24 hours, depending on the weather and the freshness of the plaster. If after 24 hours the plaster is still damp or crumbly then it was out of date and should be discarded — time to start again! (Art suppliers are generally a reliable source of small quantities. I suggest you buy plaster in bulk only if you take up casting and mould making.) To be on the safe side, always keep a packet of Spackle or tube of plaster repairer on the workbench. This way you

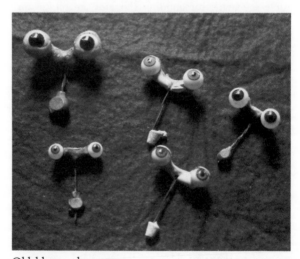

Old blown glass eyes

Assortment of eyes from Pedigree and celluloid hush-a-bye dolls

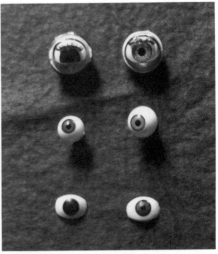

Modern eyes, found in plastic and reproduction dolls. The reproduction glass sleeping eyes now available are often used, but are very costly

won't have to go traipsing off in the middle of a job to buy more plaster.

If you have to set the eyes all over again, clean out all the plaster from the doll's head using a brush and spatula. Wipe off the eyes, remove and discard the Blu-tack, clean and wipe out the inside of the head. Allow to dry out before beginning again, replacing Vaseline and Blu-tack.

Once the plaster has set hard, test that it has adhered to the inside of the head with a crochet hook or bamboo skewer. Remove the Blu-tack. Turn the head over and test that the eyes open and shut freely. Use cotton buds to clean Vaseline from the coloured parts of the eyes. If any excess plaster has seeped through it can easily be wiped away or freed with a needle or toothpick. If the plaster mix is thick enough this will never happen.

14 Endnotes

There are so many more things I would like to tell you before saying good-bye. Perhaps because I have shared something with you, I feel as if we have come to know each other a little. Dolls can bring a lot of joy to many people — many of mine have been loaned for exhibitions where they have been seen by old people as well as children. Children are often amazed that these dolls were the toys of their parents or grandparents. When you think about it you also will be amazed. Can you imagine the result if many of today's children were given these fragile dolls to play with? Old people are delighted to see the dolls that they played with and cherished as children.

There is much more I would like to share — advanced methods of bisque restoration, waxing techniques, soft toy restoration. Most of all I would like to write about the people I have met and the stories behind them. Some restorations have heart-warming stories behind them, some very sad ones, while others have been very humorous — like the day a very large police sergeant came down the path. My heart stood still — what dreadful news was he bearing? Moments later he stood framed in the doorway, clutching in the crook of his arm a tiny bedraggled teddy bear in desperate need of TLC.

I hope you will enjoy putting your newfound skills to the best possible use. I know what happiness and pride you will feel when someone says 'thank you' for the doll you have saved.

Final touches

Assortment of clothing, c.1920

60

Christening dress worn by a lucky German doll of 1920

Reproductions made from altar boy's top

A set of hand-sewn silk replica clothing made from a wedding dress in 1930

Silk and satin reproductions

Where to find things

Art shops
UHU glue
Aquadhere
Selleys Porcelain Repair Kit
Araldite 5-minute adhesive
Moulding wax
Arbee cold moulding latex
Rubber resin
Barbola
Wire
Plaster of Paris
Gesso
Kaolin
Formalin solution
Oil paints
Acrylic paints
Brushes

Hardware stores
Selleys Porcelain Repair Kit
Plasti-Bond
Araldite 5-minute adhesive
Sandpaper
Long-nosed pliers
Small pliers
Wire

Plaster of Paris
String
Split pins
S-hooks
Porcelain filler

Chemists
Surgical scissors
Vaseline
Oxy-10

Dental suppliers
Vertex SC self curing compound
Acrylic tooth filler

Ceramic studios
Mayco bisque stains

Furniture manufacturers
Wood sawdust

Supermarkets
Dry cleaning fluid
Baby oil
Rubber bands
Gelatine
Nifty cleanser

Cotton filling
Bamboo skewers
Blu-tack

Specialists
Paper clay
Paper Clay Products
1/17 Kingsford St, Fairy Meadows
NSW 2519

Doll-related items
Lambton Hobby Ceramics
43A Dickson St, Lambton NSW 2299
Porcelain doll parts, stringing elastic,
eyes, wigs, eyelashes, Duncan's matte
spray and Duncan's flesh waterpaint,
spatulas, brushes

Museum
Romy Roeder
2 Badgery St, Lawson NSW 2617
(047) 59-1516
A lover of old dolls, Romy is always
happy to assist. Her museum,
containing many dolls, bears, and toys
of all descriptions, will captivate and
inspire you

Index

Bakelite compositions, 42
Biro marks, removing from dolls, 10
Bisque
  alternative repair materials, 41
  finger repairs, 39
  Mayco bisque stains, 55
  painting with oils, 55
  plaster moulds for missing parts, 40
  repairs, 34, 37, 39–41
  repairing holes, 39, 40
  repairing with kaolin, 34, 39, 40
Celluloid
  glueing, 44, 45
  painting, 56
  removing dents from, 44
  repairing with Araldite, 44, 45
Celluloid dolls
  cracks and splits at the joints, 45
  nose replacement, 45, 46
  repairing, 44–6
  replacing fingers, 46
  restringing, 49–53
Cherub repairs, 42, 43
Cleaning plastic dolls, 9
Cloth bodies, replacing cloth bodies on modern plastic
  dolls, 11–16
Clothing for dolls, 60–2
Composition
  filling scratches with Aquadhere, 33
  repairing and building up, 29–32
  repairing sawdust-based composition, 29
  repairing with Plasti-Bond, 32, 33
  replacing a broken or missing finger, 30–2
  sanding repairs, 29
Composition dolls
  painting, 54, 55
  repairing crazed paintwork, 55
  restringing, 24–8
Drying frames for painting, 56
Eyes, resetting sleeping eyes, 57–9
Finger repairs, 18, 30–2, 39, 42, 43, 46
Finishing dolls with baby oil, 9
Gesso, repairing with, 33, 38
Hair, see also Wigs
  brushing and setting dolls' hair, 19–21
  cleaning and restoring a nylon wig, 19–21

  human hair wigs, 21
  mohair wigs, 21
  restoring dolls' hair, 19–23
  washing dolls' hair, 19–21
Materials, where to find them, 63
Nose replacement in celluloid doll, 45, 46
Painting dolls, 54–6
  bisque, 55
  celluloid, 56
  colour matching, 54
  composition, 54, 55
  composition doll with crazed paintwork,
    55
  drying frames, 56
  eyes and lips, 55
  materials, 54
  painting blush areas, 55
  Pedigree-type dolls, 56
  repainting whole dolls, 56
Papier-mâché, repairing, 32, 33
Pedigree repairs, 42, 43
Pedigree-type dolls, painting, 56
Plaster, repairing, 32, 33
Plastic dolls
  assembling dolls without grooves, 12–15
  cleaning and rejuvenating, 9
  finger repairs, 42, 43
  finishing with baby oil, 9
  making a new cloth body, 11, 12
  removing biro marks, 10, 17
  repairing with Vertex, 42, 43
  replacing cloth bodies on modern dolls, 11–16
  replacing the head on a cloth body, 15, 16
Restringing, 35, 36
  celluloid dolls, 49–53
  composition dolls, 24–8
  resetting hooks with plaster, 28
  restringing hooks, 24
  selecting elastic, 24, 49
Sleeping eyes, resetting, 57–9
Supporting repairs while they dry, 45
Vinyl dolls, see Plastic dolls
Wigs, see also Hair
  fixing a wig permanently, 22, 23
  removing old wigs, 21, 22
  washing and cleaning, 19–21